Tapping for Teachers

"Relieve the Stress and Go for Success"

A Workbook for Personal and Professional Achievement

Elizabeth Solana Calabro, CHt.

Copyright © 2014 by Elizabeth Solana Calabro

Solana Press

All rights reserved. No part of this book may be reproduced by any mechanical, photographic, or electronic process, or in the form of a phonographic recording; nor may it be stored in a retrieval system, transmitted, or otherwise be copied for public or private use –other than for "fair use" as brief quotations embodied in articles and reviews-without written permission for the author.

The author of this book does not dispense medical advice or prescribe the use of any technique as a form of treatment for physical, emotional, or medical problems without the advice of a physician. In the event you use any of the information in this book for yourself, the author assumes no responsibility for your actions.

Publisher's Note:

While the author has made every effort to provide accurate website addresses at the time of publication neither the publisher or author assumes any responsibility for content, errors or for changes that occur after publication.

Soft cover ISBN- 978-0-9914945-0-7
Digital ISBN- 978-0-9914945-1-4

DEDICATION

To Kate

CONTENTS

	Introduction	1
Chapter 1	Tapping, You and Stress	3
Chapter 2	The Tapping Process	7
Chapter 3	How to Tap	17
Chapter 4	In the Classroom or at Home	21
Chapter 5	When Working with Children	25
Chapter 6	Resources	29

ACKNOWLEDGMENTS

Thank you to…..
My students who taught me patience and understanding.
My mentors, colleagues, trainers and instructors who modeled effective teaching practices and shared their knowledge, expertise and experience. And of course to those EFT practitioners who tirelessly spread the word and help those around them rid themselves of
"Limiting beliefs".

INTRODUCTION

Tapping is fantastic, unbelievable and gives results!!!

What if you had a way to calm down, focus, alleviate stress and deal with anxiety, fear and tension, quickly and easily? What if you could think more clearly and make mental connections more quickly? What if your day-to-day tasks become more fluid, natural and clear? What if you can help your students achieve beyond their expectations? What if you had a method so basic that you carry the tools in your fingertips? Tapping can do all of this for you.

What is Emotional Freedom Technique (Tapping)?
EFT is a simple way to balance your body's energy; to help relax and release negative emotions or stress that may be impacting your wellness or your ability to perform to your full capabilities. By "Tapping" on particular spots on the body, which are based on acupuncture/acupressure points, and repeating specific, focused phrases, one releases stress by effecting change in the chemical and physiological structure of the body, thus creating relaxation and calmness. When you are calm, clear and no longer in a stress mode, you are better able to deal with life and the classroom.

The principle behind EFT is that all negative emotions are caused by disruptions in the body's energy system, and as we know, our unresolved emotions and past traumas contribute to our physical ailments, performance and behaviors. EFT clears these disruptions and unresolved emotions through stimulating points along the body's energy meridians. By holding a situation or memory in mind while repeating specific statements and at the same time tapping on points of the body that correspond to acupressure meridians, we can balance the body's energy.

Tapping will change your life. You are faced with an ever-changing environment in the classroom. Your students enter each day, bringing with them their personal thoughts, challenges and anxieties but also their emotions, which are influenced by the demands of school and home. Educators have a challenging career. The demands and expectations are high, as they should be, but unless you as the leader in the classroom can manage stress and create an environment of success, your efforts will NOT meet your expectations. This isn't news to you.

Tapping on any issue will make you more at ease, comfortable and effective as the leader (facilitator) in your world. Tapping is a tool that will prepare you to be most effective in creating a positive environment, handle day-to-day events and enable you and your students to function at the highest levels possible.

It's natural to tap. Do you tap on your chin or temple when you are thinking? Do you rub your temple or forehead when you are tired or stressed? Do you tap your finger when problem-solving? We need to rethink our reaction to a student's tapping pencil as they are solving a problem or reading a book.

"Sounds like it's too good to be true...why haven't I heard of this before? If it's so great why doesn't everyone know about it?" you may ask. EFT has been around for over 40 years. The process is based on the work of Dr. John Diamond, Roger Callahan and Gary Craig. Mr. Craig offered his interpretation and refinement of the process to the world. Studies show that Tapping has had a positive affect on student performance in the classroom and on the athletic field. Personally, I wish I had heard about it earlier in my 34-year teaching career. Once I did learn this simple process, I used it. It definitely works. You don't even have to believe it for it to work. It just works.

This book is an introduction to the tapping process. It is meant for you to personally learn and use, for your own benefit. Although the title refers to teachers, everyone will benefit from Tapping. Are we not all teachers, in a sense?

CHAPTER 1
TAPPING, YOU AND STRESS

In any real or perceived stressful situation our primitive alarm system goes off; fight, flight or freeze. Adrenaline is pumping. You are on high alert. Well that is fine if you are in real danger, but sometimes having to stand in front of a group of people, give a presentation, problem-solve a conflict situation, or meet a dead-line (by the way, we as teachers do all these things everyday) can create those same primitive reactions. Not so great for the body or mind.

On a day-to-day basis, as the facilitator of the classroom (conference room, boardroom, locker room or field), you are faced with a variety and range of emotions, reactions and temperaments. You need to be prepared academically, organize and manage a group of children (teens or adults), perform, evaluate, negotiate, coordinate, create and execute a lesson and at the same time be evaluated by supervisors. Talk about STRESS. Your success in educating (leading, coaching, or directing) will depend on your state of mind/body. The way you feel, your attitude, emotions and energy will set the tone of your classroom environment.

Why should you use Tapping?
Tapping rapidly reduces the impact of incidents that trigger emotional distress. Once the distress is reduced or removed, the body will often rebalance itself, and accelerate to a state of wellbeing, confidence and calm.

Tapping can create the same effects on the body as meditation does, but in much less time.

Tapping is:
A tool to help deal with emotion, fear and anxiety.
A tool to calm, focus and clear the mind and body.
A tool to reach a state of peak performance.

Use Tapping on yourself. Do this for yourself. Your emotional issues will be released therefore you will be present in your interactions with the people around you. Tapping will help you to create an environment best suited to cooperation, collaboration and innovation. You set the tone and environment in the area(s) you manage, your classroom. Your energy becomes your student's energy. Tapping (EFT) will help you be more present in the classroom, able to handle any situation clear-headed, calm and efficiently. I'm not the only teacher who has used Tapping. Look at the resource page for video links and ideas from teachers who Tap.

The goal is:
To remain calm.
Set the emotional environment best suited for success for you and the children you work with.
To give yourself and the child/teenager a sense of empowerment.

Tapping can help you with the following issues and topics:

- Professional Performance-class leadership, organization and presentation of material, classroom management and time management.
- Test Anxiety & Stress
- Public Speaking and Presentations
- Observations and Conferences-parent/teacher, teacher/administrator, peer to peer
- Focus and Attention
- School Performance (yours' and your students')
- Sports Anxiety & Performance
- Learning Difficulties
- Self-esteem
- Peer Relationships and Bullying
- Confidence
- Phobias & Fears
- Nightmares
- Sleep Problems
- Emotional Distress-anger, frustration, loneliness
- Coping Strategies

This process has been expanded upon, revised and further developed by psychiatrists, psychologists, engineers and scientists. There have been success stories for those with fears, anxieties, PTSD, ailments, sleep issues, weight gain, smoking...well the list goes on and on. There is now scientific evidence that shows how this process affects the body. I'm not here to rewrite all that information. The extensive bibliography has resources for you to explore. I know you are busy and I've already taken up much of your valuable time, so let's get to the process.

Note: Should you find the emotion, stress or situation to be beyond your tapping limits, I highly recommend you seek a certified EFT practitioner.

NOTES:

CHAPTER 2
THE TAPPING PROCESS

This is for YOU. Learn this process; use it and I hope you choose to share it. You are part of a movement for change in your classroom and eventually in the world. When this process works for you, and it will, you will affect those who interact with you. Whether or not you incorporate this process into your classroom (boardroom, playing field, home or office) activities is entirely up to you...but I firmly believe that your personal participation in this amazing practice will make a huge difference for you and will indirectly influence the achievements of those around you. Tap on a daily basis. Use this practice before events, which may be stressful to you. Use it at any time you need to.

Scenario:

You feel anxiety rising in every part of your body...you anticipate a stressful situation. Maybe the event is a parent meeting, your lesson/class presentation, an exam you must take or any one of the million-plus experiences of life. The feelings are powerful. Your reactions are not helpful to you: heart beating quickly, fuzzy thoughts, not able to focus, stomach in knots, and heat running throughout your body. The feeling may grow stronger each moment, to the point of stopping you from doing your best.

It's time to Tap.

Step 1- Identify the feeling and the emotions.

A) What are you feeling? Are you sad, fearful, angry, and disappointed? Sometimes it begins with the emotion; sometimes it begins with the thought of the event.

Ask yourself if that feeling is presenting itself somewhere in your body.

Do you feel anything in your body? Discomfort, pain or un-ease?

What does it feel like and where do you feel it? Is it heaviness in your shoulders? A tightness in your chest, a swirling motion in your stomach? A pain in your back or head or numbness in your fingertips? Does it feel like it's hard to breathe or as if you are stuck, frozen, unable to move, speak or think?

B) **Ask yourself the following questions and be specific in your answers.** Write it down-these are the words you will use to create your set up phrase later in Step 4. Be honest; just go with whatever comes to mind.

   a. What is bugging you?

   b. How do you feel? What are the emotions?

   c. Where in your body do you feel it? What sensations are you feeling?

Step 2-Rank the emotion/feeling you are feeling.

This is your individual scale of measurement. It is named a SUD (Subjective Unit of Distress). This number has meaning to you. 10 represents the worst and 0 is the best you can feel. One of my clients stated that her number was 564----a young, stressed and overwhelmed parent of two toddlers!
Circle any number between 0 and 10.

0	1	2	3	4	5	6	7	8	9	10

Step 3-Getting to the core issue or event. Close your eyes and create a movie in your mind of the first time you felt these feelings, disruption or stress. Do you sense the aromas, hear the sounds, and feel the feeling of the event? You may be surprised to find that the image in your mind is from a long time ago, really has nothing to do with what you are facing today (or anticipating). It may seem strange that this event has come to mind, but just go with it. This may be the past Core Issue, the reason why you react the way you do today.

Write it down- perhaps the words are different then before, more to the point, more clear, more painful. These are the words you will use to create your set up phrases in Step 4.

a. What is bugging you?

b. How do you feel? What are the emotions?

c. Where do you feel it? What sensations are you feeling?

At this point you may also find that your SUD ranking has changed. If it has, circle your level here now.

0	1	2	3	4	5	6	7	8	9	10

Step 4-Creating your set up phrases-Getting to the Core Issue.

Now you may be feeling more stress then when you began the process, but that's OK. It's a good thing, because you are addressing the core problem or issue. The trigger that is activated to produce discomfort will be released and eliminated. You are going to tap it out, feel a wonderful sense of relief and that THING, whatever it is, will no longer cause you to react in a self defeating way.

You will create three phrases based on the answers you have previously written. Looking back at the words describing your feelings and the physical and/or emotional reactions that you wrote down in Steps 1-3, choose those that are most emotional. These are your **key words**. Fill in the blank spaces in the phrases with those key words.

NOTE: At this point you may add to/or change your words. The key to success is getting to the core issue, the true words, and the real feelings.

Fill in the spaces:

Even though _____(fill in the blank with the feeling, emotion or circumstances of the event), I totally and completely LOVE AND ACCEPT MYSELF.

Even though _____(fill in the blank with the feeling, emotion or circumstances of the event), I totally and completely LOVE AND ACCEPT MYSELF.

Even though _____(fill in the blank with the feeling, emotion or circumstances of the event), I totally and completely LOVE AND ACCEPT MYSELF.

Step 5-Tap on the side of your hand, like a Karate Chop, as you repeat your three phrases.

Step 6-Tap gently on the body tapping points, as you repeat just your **key words** from the phrases. See Chapter 3 for specific points and instruction.

Step 7-Rank your level of intensity. Test yourself--Think of that event and replay the movie in your mind. Go back to that first time.
How do you feel?

0	1	2	3	4	5	6	7	8	9	10

At this point you will find that your SUD ranking has changed.

If your SUDS level has not fallen below a 3, repeat Steps 5 and 6 using the phrase on the next page. The words **"I Still"** have been added to this round of Tapping.

NOTE: You may also find other words/emotions come to mind. If that is the case, use them and know that being emotional or over the top in the words you use is OK, as long as these words are true for you.

Even though, I **still** _____(fill in the blank with the feeling, emotion or circumstances of the event), I totally and completely LOVE AND ACCEPT MYSELF.

Even though, I **still** _____(fill in the blank with the feeling, emotion or circumstances of the event), I totally and completely LOVE AND ACCEPT MYSELF.

Even though, I **still**_____(fill in the blank with the feeling, emotion or circumstances of the event), I totally and completely

THE STEPS MAY LOOK LIKE THIS:

Scenario: You are confident in your classroom and have wonderful rapport with your students. You are organized and know the materials thoroughly. Your kids are usually engaged and interested. You know that you have prepared a great new lesson. You are presenting that new lesson in class today. Your supervisor has left you a note that he/she plans to stop by today. THIS IS THE FIRST VISIT OF THE YEAR. You have no idea what time? Will it be during that new lesson? Your mind begins to race: "What if the kids don't respond to the lesson?" "What if I get flustered, and what if Jane or Joe acts up?" "What if the kids just look at me like they don't get it? What if the kids really don't understand me? What if my supervisor doesn't get it? What if I rush through this? What if I speak too quickly?"

What If? What If? What If? Those self doubts and feelings of anxiety surface and you don't understand why these terrible feelings and these emotions are taking over your body/mind.

Now it's your time to Tap.

Step 1-Identify the feeling.

A) What am I feeling?
"I am feeling disappointed in my self, nervous and fearful."

Ask yourself if that feeling is presenting itself somewhere in your body now. Do you feel anything in your body?

GET IN TOUCH WITH YOUR BODY NOW!

"STOMACH IS ACHING
FEEL A TIGHTNESS IN THROAT"

B) Ask yourself the following questions and be specific in your answers. Be honest; just go with whatever comes to mind. Write it down-These are the words you will use to create your set up phrase later in Step 4.

a. **What is bugging (or bothering) you?** *"I'm nervous about what my supervisor will think about my lesson. I think it's a good lesson but I have never presented it before, it's something new."*

b. **How do you feel?** *"FEEL stuck, unable to think clearly."*

c. **Where do you feel it?** *"It's in my head, tightness in my throat and stomach."*

Step 2-Rank the level of discomfort that emotion or feeling is giving you. Any number between 0 and 10.

10 is the worst - 0 (zero) feeling the best.
This is the SUD (Subjective Unit of Discomfort).

The SUDS in this situation is 8.

0	1	2	3	4	5	6	7	8

Step 3-Getting to the core issue or event.

When did you **first** feel this way? Close your eyes and let your mind wander. Create or just imagine a movie in your mind.

To your amazement, you are back in elementary school, standing in front of your classmates ready to present your "Show and Tell". YOU FORGOT ABOUT THE ASSIGNMENT THAT DAY AND JUST GRABED A TOY. You are usually happy in class. You get along with your classmates and love school most of the time. This is something new, you didn't prepare enough, standing in front of everyone is scary, and you never really liked speaking in front of the class. Everyone has finished presenting and you are the last student to speak. They have cool stuff. The day is almost done; you have 2 minutes to present. As the day went on and the other students were "showing and telling" your stomach began to hurt, you couldn't focus because all you heard in your head was, "Please pick me now. What if the kids laugh? All I have is that stupid toy. What if I stumble, fall on my face? Why isn't she picking me?"

WOW! WHERE DID THAT COME FROM?
WHAT DOES THAT HAVE TO DO WITH TODAY?

Now ask yourself those questions again. Focus on the long ago event. Write down whatever comes to mind: The words may be different.
   a. **What is bugging or bothering you?**

   When will I be picked to present?
   She's making me wait.
   The other kids are done. They will laugh at me.
   I want to go home. I can't do this.
   The kids are going to laugh at me. What if I get stuck or stutter?
   What if they don't like my stuff?

   b. **How do you feel?** *Scared, sick, AFRAID.*

   c. **Where do you feel it?** *My head aches, my throat is tight, my* *stomach hurts.*

At this point ask yourself to rank your emotions, again. The SUD (Subjective Unit of Discomfort). SUDS-is now 9/10

0	1	2	3	4	5	6	7	8	**9**	**10**

Step 4-Creating your set up phrase-Getting to the core of the issue.

YOU WILL CREATE 3 PHRASES BASED ON THE MOVIE in your mind. Use the <u>words and feelings</u> from the questions you just answered. Choose words/phrases that have the greatest affect on you.

Even though __*SHE DIDN'T PICK ME, my stomach aches*___, I totally and completely LOVE AND ACCEPT MYSELF.

Even though_ *I'M AFRAID TO STUMBLE, stutter, I'm scared*__, I totally and completely LOVE AND ACCEPT MYSELF.

Even though _*THEY WILL LAUGH AT ME, I can't speak*___, I totally and completely LOVE AND ACCEPT MYSELF.

Step 5-Tap on the Karate Chop, at the same time repeating each of the set-up phrases 3 times.

Step 6-Key Words-Tap gently on each of the body tapping spots (Chapter 3) as you repeat just your **key words** from the phrases.

Key words are the words that have the most emotional trigger for you.
"Laugh at me"   "Stumble"   "Can't Speak"   "Scared" "Afraid"

Step 7-Test yourself--Think of that event from long ago and replay the movie.

How do you feel? What is your level of discomfort? Rank your SUD.

The Suds level has gone down, but tapping again will be helpful.

0	1	2	3	**4**	5	6	7	8	9	10

If your SUD is not below the number 3, tap again beginning from Step 4 and include the word STILL in the set up phrase:

Even though She **still**, *DIDN'T PICK ME, my stomach aches*, I totally and completely LOVE AND ACCEPT MYSELF.

Even though I'M **still** *AFRAID TO STUMBLE, I'm scared*, I totally and completely LOVE AND ACCEPT MYSELF.

Even though THEY **still** *LAUGH AT ME, I CAN'T SPEAK*, I totally and completely LOVE AND ACCEPT MYSELF.

Test yourself again--Think of that event again and replay the movie in your mind.

What is the level of discomfort? SUD

0	**1**	2	3	4	5	6	7	8	9	10

Getting to the core issue is key to success.
Did something else come to mind? If so go back to the beginning of the process and complete each step.

How do you feel? There is a level of relief, perhaps a sigh, it's easier to breathe and the thought of that event is not producing the same physical effect. The trigger is not firing. You may even be a little surprised, feeling a sense of freedom, clarity and understanding. You are not triggered by the thought and no matter how hard you attempt to get to that stressed place, it is not happening for you.

It's your turn now. Create your set up phrase and then follow the tapping sequence in the next chapter. You will find a "Set-Up Phrase Worksheet" at the end of this book. For ultimate success in this process, you must be open to and go with what ever comes to mind.

Notes:

CHAPTER 3
HOW TO TAP

Have you created your set up phrases using the worksheet at the end of this book? Once you have created your set up phrases, you are ready to begin Tapping. Begin tapping with **The Karate Chop**. The idea is to tap the side of one hand, against the open palm of the other hand, like a Karate chop.

Please note these very important tips:
- You may use either hand to tap.
- You may use both hands, if you choose.
- Tapping is gentle, unless you feel a higher level of force needs to be expressed due to your emotion.
- Tapping should not cause pain or bruising.

Karate Chop
Let's tap the Karate Chop. As you repeat each set up phrase three (3) times, gently tap of the side of your hand.

Even though _____(fill in the blank with the feeling, emotion or circumstances of the event), I totally and completely LOVE AND ACCEPT MYSELF.

Even though _____(fill in the blank with the feeling, emotion or circumstances of the event), I totally and completely LOVE AND ACCEPT MYSELF.

Even though_____(fill in the blank with the feeling, emotion or circumstances of the event), I totally and completely LOVE AND ACCEPT MYSELF.

Tapping the Body

Identify your **key words**, the emotions, feelings, and the stuff that is bothering you. These are the words you used in your Set-up phrases. Choose the words that had the most effect on you as you Karate Chopped, the word(s) that gave you a charge or intensified emotion. Write them down, below.

Key Words:

_____, _____, _____

You will repeat a key word as you tap. Using two or three fingers, tap 5 to 8 times gently on your body beginning at the top of the head down to your sore spots.

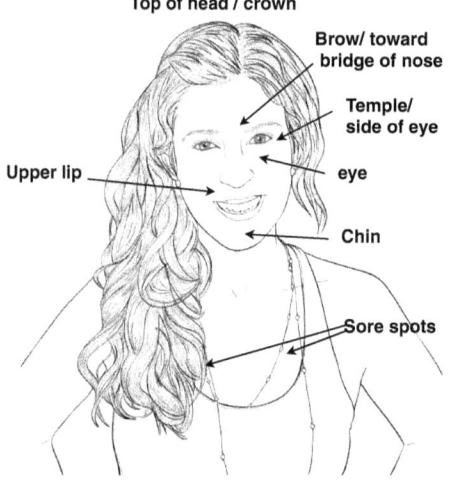

Tapping spots
Top of head.

Brow-toward the bridge of your nose, right on the eyebrow.

Temple-on the side of your eye, you can feel the eye socket bone. Tap very gently.

Under Eye-at the center of the eye on the socket bone.

Upper lip-use the pads of your fingers, tap on the center of the upper lip.

Chin-use the pads of your fingers tap on the center of the chin.

Sore Spots-located about 3 inches down and 3 inches to the left and right of the collarbone.

Additional tapping spots:
1) Under the arm
2) Across the wrist
3) Under breast-across the bottom of the rib cage

Always check your SUD level when you complete a round of tapping

0	1	2	3	4	5	6	7	8	9	10

(from head down).

Circle your SUD Level - 0 to 10

Repeat the process saying the phrases, including the word "still," if your numbers do not go down.

The Super Spot
There are times when tapping all over your body may not be appropriate, because of where you are or what you are doing. You may not feel comfortable tapping your head while standing in front of your class or in a conference. There is an alternative. I call it the Super Spot. It is a quick, go-to spot that will help you to relax, focus and remain calm.

The Super Spot
Take your hand and place it straight across the center of your chest with your index finder touching your sternum (boney protrusion at base of the neck). Tap your pinky. That tapping point is your Super Spot. When you tap gently on this spot, with your

whole hand or just your fingertips, your body begins to produce "feel good" natural chemicals.

You may repeat the entire "set-up phrase", individual key trigger word(s) or nothing at all. Perhaps this is a spot you naturally go to in times of stress or when solving a problem. You may notice college and professional athletes tap while setting up the shot or while on the bench between plays.

The Super Spot is extremely powerful, easy to tap and not noticeable to others. Tap this spot everyday.

CHAPTER 4
IN THE CLASSROOM OR AT HOME

Tapping has been incorporated into classrooms throughout the world. Canadian teachers Erin Ness and Marlise Widdershoven created a Tapping Space in their classroom where children can go when they feel frustrated and need to compose themselves. This area includes a computer program, which allows the children to identify their feelings, tap on a stuffed animal and calm themselves down.

Marlise introduces tapping before testing to help her students relax, focus and build confidence. She made it fun by naming it the **Crazy Dance**. The kids repeat affirmations as they tap and dance around the room. Listen to the enthusiasm, energy and insight expressed by these two young teachers for yourself: EFT in Schools. http://www.blogtalkradio.com/eftradio/2009/05/13/eft-for-schools

Till Shilling, a pharmacist read about the effects of EFT on blood panels and although skeptical at first, become involved in training and sharing this technique throughout the world. He created Tappy Bear, a stuffed bear with tapping points on it, specifically designed to help parents/adults assist children in dealing with their emotions and feelings. Although Tappy Bear is no longer in production, Till continues to spread the word about EFT in schools throughout South America (www.tillschilling.com in Spanish).

Karin Davidson, EFT Trainer, Matrix Reimprinting Trainer and Co-Author of EFT Certification course-books has created the "Feel Better Buddies". These are an assortment of stuffed animals with embroidered tapping points, made for adults to assist children with tapping. You can find these tools and instructional DVD's on her website. www.feelbetterbuddies.com

Jondi Whitis and Sue Hubbard Tarlton have created a wonderful resource, Tapping Star, www.tappingstar.com. This is an organization dedicated to encouraging the use of EFT in the classroom. The website has a wealth of information and handouts for classroom use, in addition to videos of kids in tapping action.

Should you decide to introduce this technique to your students or use it with your own children at home, make this a fun experience.

I have included a few approaches to tapping in the classroom. Perhaps you will tap as a group prior to a new activity, quiz or lesson.

Tap Hello - A powerful way start the day or to transition from one subject or activity to another. I found this particular technique useful in working with middle school students, moving from class to class, who needed to focus and release any negative energy or thoughts before the next unit or class begins. There is no need for words, just a calm atmosphere.

1. Student sits crossing one leg over the other with their ankle resting on their knee (either left ankle on right knee or right ankle on left knee).
2. Place the opposite hand on the ankle resting on your knee (left hand resting on right ankle or right hand resting on left ankle). You have created an electrical circuit with your body.
3. Place your tongue on the roof of your mouth.
4. Eyes can be open or closed.
5. Tap on the "super spot" for 30 to 60 seconds.
If you have a timer use it.

Simon Says- Play a game of "Simon Says" or "Monkey See, Monkey Do" using the tapping spots. Include affirmations or positive messages as you do.

Simon Says:
Simon says, "Tap on your brow as you repeat, I love to have fun."
Simon says, "Tap on your brow as you repeat, I'm a great kid."
Simon says, "Tap on your chin as you repeat, I'm strong."

The Secret Tap- (adaption of the 9-gamut) is a hand tapping activity that can be done anywhere. It is not noticeable and it is a natural tapping motion. It can be done with your hand placed above or below the desk, beneath one hand or behind your back.

Using the thumb gently tap, 8 times on the side of your fingers. Tap on the joint close to the fingernail. (The spot is pointed out in the diagram below).

- Tap the index finger
- Tap the second finger
- Skip the ring finger
- Tap the pinky
- Using your index finger tap the side of the thumb
- Repeat

Note: A variation is to use both hands at the same time.

EFT Shortcut-Mary E. Stafford, M.Ed., L.P.C. offers the following tapping shortcut for children.

1. Tap all over the top of the head with the fingers of one hand.
2. With the flat of the hand tap on the chest in the center below the collarbone. (Super Spot)
3. With the flat of one hand, tap on the inside of the wrist.

4. With the flat of one hand tap above the ankle bone on the inside of the leg.

Mary says that children become relaxed when otherwise tense and that this process is good for addressing test anxiety.

When to Tap:
- Tap at the beginning of the day.
- Tap before a test, a quiz or a spelling bee.
- Tap before public speaking, book report or class presentations.
- Tap before a practice, performance or athletic event.
- Tap while listening to presentations, lectures, and instructions or during a pop quiz.
- Tap for creativity-goal setting, problem solving or brainstorming sessions.
- Tap during a group activity or project.
- Tap before competitions.
- Tap while reading or completing homework.
- Preventive tapping focusing on the future. Prepare yourself for the ever-changing climate in the classroom and your world.

May I also suggest that you look into the work of Donna Eden. The book, The *Promise of Energy Medicine,* includes chapters describing the role of the body's energy system and how through movement and activity you can create a more balanced, positive and productive energy field within your body. Exercises include the cross crawl and zip up, among others. In addition Carla Hannaford's, Ph.D. *Smart Moves-Why Learning Is Not All In Your Head* is an excellent resource of the how's and why's of energy, movement and learning.

Another wonderful resource is Brain Gym®, a series of programs designed for children, includes specific exercises addressing the needs and demands of the classroom. Gail and Paul E. Dennison have developed comprehensive curriculum and materials, incorporating movement and motion that helps the child focus and relax.

CHAPTER 5
WHEN WORKING WITH CHILDREN

Children are highly perceptive of your emotions and attitudes. Your level of ease, calmness and manor of speaking will have a positive or negative influence on those around you. You set the tone and the level of expectation in your classroom. For this reason you should enter the classroom prepared to handle any situation. Tapping on yourself is highly recommended before you begin the day interacting with others. Get yourself to a place of openness and relaxation before anyone walks into your room.

Keep in mind that levels of anxiety vary in each child, where as one situation may not affect one child, that same situation or environment may trigger an emotional reaction in another child. When anyone is put into a real or perceived stressful situation a primitive alarm system goes off. In the case of a child the following also holds true:

- Reality does not exist in the same way it does for an adult.
- Children will react to your emotions. The same way laughter is contagious, so is anxiousness and stress.
- Children are very perceptive of emotions. Although they may not be able to attribute the cause, they tend to blame themselves for what is happening.

When you are dealing with a child one on one, make sure that you are calm. Calm yourself first (tap on the super spot) and then work with the child. It's like being on an airplane. When the air mask drops down, you place it over your mouth first and then give it to the child. It's the same idea, when you are dealing with kids, you are better able to handle the situation, when you are calm and express it.

Suggestions when working with kids:

Keep in mind that your behavior and feelings will directly affect the child.
Don't be anxious about their problem.
Get rapport; physically go to their level. Bend down.
Always treat the child with respect.
Acknowledge the child's feelings and emotions:
"You look sad"
"You seem to be mad"

Use simple language, words that make sense to a child. Instead of ending the phases with "I totally and completely LOVE AND ACCEPT MYSELF" use:
...I'm a great kid.
...I am fun.
...I can do this.

Explain to the child that tapping on these special spots, helps them to feel better, calm down, make better choices, think more clearly or remember more.

One-on-One
When a child has an issue and is distressed in the classroom, simply giving the child attention will help to calm them down. Listen to the child's story and ask them to start tapping or you begin to tap on yourself, as they tell you about what is upsetting them. Remain neutral; simply LISTEN, without reaction or judgment. Encourage the child to tap until they have finished telling you their story.
At the end of their story, ask the question:
What is upsetting you the most now?

Continue to listen as the child tells you what is upsetting them most. Within a few minutes of tapping it is likely that the anger/fear/anxiety they felt before they started tapping, has been significantly reduced.

A Tapping Place

One-on-one attention more likely will not be possible at all times. Having a designated place in the classroom where the child could go to process these feeling would be wonderful. Create a **Tapping Place** not a "time-out space". Make this space comfortable, have a stuffed animal the child can hold (and tap on) and/or a visual, either video or print that guides the child in tapping it out. Perhaps you have soothing music and earphones available. The child should feel welcome and not consider this as a punishment in any way, just a place to go to calm down and feel better. Teens could benefit from this same type of set-up. Develop clear guidelines or rules for this "Tapping Place". Use a timer to control time away from the rest of the class. Have typical key TRIGGER words posted on the wall. Use a room divider or half wall to make the "Tapping Place" private.

MY TWO CENTS:

In my experience as an educator, the circumstances that cause a child to be in distress or disruptive in the classroom, in most cases, stem from the child's frustration, fears, self-doubt or confusion, either based on home or classroom experiences.

Tapping is highly effective in helping the child move past those feelings, calm down and become more open to listening and participating in the classroom. In addition to calming students, you will find that creativity, attention and productivity will increase, with the use of this fantastic technique. You are giving your students a tool that will be of value for the rest of their lives.

NOTES:

CHAPTER 6
RESOURCES

TAPPING FOR TEACHERS - www.tapforteachers.com
　A website and resource for this workbook.
Please, sign up for **tapping reminders**…tapping doesn't work if you don't remember to do it. I will send you an occasional reminder to tap.

TAP TO ACHIEVE-.　www.taptoachieve.com
　A blog with tips and techniques for the effective teacher and student. Join the conversation; share your successes and suggestions.

Look for more info:
FACEBOOK, look for and follow the Tapping for Teachers page.
Youtube.com –Elizabeth Calabro

Please find this **special bonus** just for you. As a huge thank you for purchasing and reading this workbook, and for being open to this wonderful technique, you will find worksheets and video training via the link below. This is just for you and you must use the special code. Enjoy.
　Tapping for Teachers worksheets and videos are available on-line.
　www.tapforteachers.com/workshop.html　(code: kate)

Workshops:
I am available for workshops, presentations, Skype or FaceTime meetings. I would love to meet you and share this wonderful technique in person.

　Please contact me:
　tapforteachers@gmail.com
　www.tapforteachers.com

Books For You

Bender, Sheila. *The Energy of Belief: Psychology's Power Tools to Focus Intention and Release Blocking Beliefs,* Energy Psychology Press; 1 edition (November 15, 2007)

Callahan, Roger. *Tapping the Healer Within: Using Thought-Field Therapy to Instantly Conquer Your Fears, Anxieties, and Emotional Distress,* McGraw-Hill; 1st edition (May 9, 2002)

Craig, Gary. *The EFT Manual (EFT: Emotional Freedom Techniques),* Energy Psychology Press; 2nd edition (March 15, 2011)

Craig, Gary, Eden, Donna & Feinstein, David. *The Promise of Energy Psychology: Revolutionary Tools for Dramatic Personal Change,* Penguin 2003

Eden, Donna. *The Little Book of Energy Medicine: The Essential Guide to Balancing Your Body's Energies;* Tarcher, 2012

Gallo, Fred & Vincenzi, Harry. *Energy Tapping: How to Rapidly Eliminate Anxiety, Depression, Cravings & More Using Energy Psychology,* New Harbinger Publications; 2nd edition (September 1, 2008)

Ortner, Nick. *The Tapping Solution: A Revolutionary System for Stress-Free Living,* Hay House, 2013

Books For or About Working with Kids

Dennison, Paul E., PhD., & Gail E. Dennison. *Brain Gym Teacher's Edition.* Edu-Kinesthetis Inc., Ventura, CA 1989

Ferreira, Jayne. *Tapping Away the Blues: You Have the Power at Your Fingertips,* CreateSpace Independent Publishing Platform (June 22, 2010)

Hannaford, Ph.D., Carla. *Smart Moves: Why Learning Is Not All in Your Head;* Great River Books; 2nd, Revised & Expanded edition (June 23, 2005)

Jeffrey Busen, Susan. *Tap into Joy: A Guide to Emotional Freedom Techniques for Kids and Their Parents,* iUniverse, Inc. (February 14, 2007)

Kay, Debbie & Ricci, Chris. *Tapping Play: Creates Your Happy Rainbow Day*, Debbie Teichmann (November 9, 2011)

Muccillo, Angie. *Tapping for Kids- A Children's Guide to EFT;* Dragonrising; 2nd edition (February 1, 2011)
http://tappingforkids.wordpress.com

Promislow, Sharon. *Making the Brain Body Connection: A Playful Guide to Releasing Mental, Physical & Emotional Blocks to Success;* Enhanced Learning & Integration; Revised edition (July 1, 2005)

Yates, Brad. *The Wizard's Wish: Or, How He Made the Yuckies Go Away - A Story About the Magic in You,* CreateSpace Independent Publishing Platform (July 24, 2010)

Websites

Tap for Teachers-online resource for this book
www.tapforteachers.com

Tap to Achieve – my blog, a resource for the effective teacher and student to get tips and suggestions that led to achievement and success. www.taptoachieve.com

EFT Blog Radio
Schoolteachers, Erin Ness and Marlise Widdershoven talk about the effectiveness of tapping as University students, teachers and how it benefits their students.
http://www.blogtalkradio.com/eftradio/2009/05/13/eft-for-schools

Tapping Star-dedicated to Tapping in School, includes complimentary handouts to use with students. Jondi Whitis and Sue Hubbard Tarlton have a goal of including EFT in classrooms across the world. They have created a turnkey school curriculum and presentations. www.tappingstar.com

EFT Radio Broadcasts via the Tapping Star
(Scroll down to the middle of the page)
http://tappingstar.ning.com/page/links-1

Test anxiety-Working with Kids
http://tappingstar.ning.com/page/downloads-1

Tapping for Kids Guide for Teachers and Parents
http://tappingforkids.wordpress.com/2008/07/15/tapping-for-kids-guide-for-teachers-and-parents/

Tapping Stuffed Animals- www.feelbetterbuddies.com

Teacher testimonials- Shakti in Hawaii, has introduced Tapping in Schools- (in Spanish)
http://www.integratedenergybalancing.com/pb/wp_a7c82b71/wp_a7c82b71.html

Tappy Bear Song in Spanish
http://www.eftmx.com/newsletter/cancion-del-osito-tappy.html

EFT Shortcut for Children. Mary Strafford PhD.
http://mindbodytherapy.com/eft_for_children.htm

Gary Craig- originator of EFT
www.emofree.com
http://www.emofree.com/eft/children.html

EFT Universe   eftuniverse.com

EFT in Spanish www.eftmx.com

The Tapping Solution www.thetappingsolution.com

On-line Videos

Brad Yates-author of the The Wizard's Wish: Or, How He Made the Yuckies Go Away - A Story About the Magic in You http://www.youtube.com/eftwizard

Jessica Ortner-The Tapping Solution-Tapping for Teachers
http://youtu.be/sMZ3KW9z0ow

Ah-hah Parenting with Dr. Laura Markham
http://www.ahaparenting.com/parenting-tools/raise-great-kids/emotionally-intelligent-child/EFT-with-kids

5 Things you Must Know Before Doing EFT with Children and Teens with Gene Monterastelli
http://tappingqanda.com/2012/03/5-things-you-must-know-before-tapping-with-children-and-teens/

EFT Videos from EFT Universe
http://www.eftuniverse.com/index.php?option=com_content&view=article&id=5&Itemid=8

Research

Benor, DJ, et al. Pilot study of emotional freedom techniques, holistic hybrid derived from eye movement desensitization and reprocessing and emotional freedom technique, and cognitive behavioral therapy for treatment of test anxiety in university students. *Explore (NY)*. 2009 Nov- Dec 5(6): 338-40.

Brattberg, G. Self-administered EFT (Emotional Freedom Techniques) in Individuals with Fibromyalgia: A Randomized Trial. *Integrative Medicine: A Clinician's Journal.* 2008 Aug/Sep; 30 -35.

Church, D et al. Psychological Trauma in Veterans using EFT (Emotional Freedom Techniques): A Randomized Controlled Trial. Presented at the 12th International Energy Psychology Conference. 2010. [in peer review].

Church, D, et al. Brief Group Intervention Using EFT (Emotional Freedom Techniques) for Depression in College Students: A Randomized Controlled Trial. Presented at the 12th International Energy Psychology Conference. 2010. [submitted for publication and in peer review].

Feinstein, D. Energy Psychology: Snake Oil or Designer Tool for Neural Change? www.eftfree.net.

Emoto, M. *Hidden Messages in Water.* 2004. Beyond Words Publishing.

Sezgin, N and Ozcan, B. The effect of progressive muscular relaxation and emotional freedom techniques on test anxiety in high school students: a randomized controlled trial. *Energy Psychology: Theory, Research, & Treatment.* 2009; 1(1); 23-30.

Stapleton, P and Sheldon, T. A Randomized Clinical Trial of a Meridian-Based Intervention for Food Cravings with Twelve Month Follow-up. *Behavior Change* [in press].

The Sport Journal #15 2012-The affect of Eft on Sports Performance
http://www.thesportjournal.org/article/sports-confidence-and-critical-incident-intensity-after-brief-application-emotional-freedom-

WORKSHEET- CREATING THE SET UP PHRASE

Step 1. Identify your feelings and emotions.
Answer the questions below. BE SPECIFIC

What is Bugging you? Close your eyes and imagine the situation. Go back to the first time you felt this way.	
How do you Feel? What are the emotions?	**Where** do you feel it in your Body? (Aches, discomfort, pain or sensations)

Step 2- Rank your feelings: Based on your level of discomfort, identify where you are on the scale below.

I feel:

0 the Best   10 the Worst

0	1	2	3	4	5	6	7	8	9	10

Step 3- Look at the words above and **Circle the three** words or phrases that give you the most negative charge (the trigger words for you).

Step 4-Creating your set-up phrases:

Complete each sentence below using the circled words. Make sure that the words are true to you.

Even though _____(fill in the blank with the feeling, emotion or circumstances of the event), I totally and completely LOVE AND ACCEPT MYSELF.

Even though _____(fill in the blank with the feeling, emotion or circumstances of the event), I totally and completely LOVE AND ACCEPT MYSELF.

Even though _____(fill in the blank with the feeling, emotion or circumstances of the event), I totally and completely LOVE AND ACCEPT MYSELF.

Step 5- Tapping – You will begin to tap on the side of your hand (Karate Chop) and at the same time repeat the set-up phrases.

Tap on the Karate Chop and repeat each phrase 3X's.

Step 6- Tap the body- Using just the key words/phrase, those words that gave you the most discomfort, tap 5-8 times on each one of the spots as indicated on diagram A.

My Key (trigger) Words are:

_____, _____, _____

Tapping spots

Top of head

Brow- toward the bridge of your nose, right on the eyebrow.

Temple- on the side of your eye, you can feel the eye socket bone. Tap very gently.

Under Eye- at the center of the eye on the socket bone.

Diagram A

Upper lip-use the pads of your fingers, tap on the center of the upper lip.

Chin-use the pads of your fingers, tap on the center of the chin.

Sore Spot- located about 3 inches down and 3 inches to the left and right of the collarbone.

Super Spot

Take your hand and place it straight across the center of your chest with your index finder touching your sternum (boney protrusion at base of the neck). Tap your pinky. That tapping point is your Super Spot.

ABOUT THE AUTHOR

Elizabeth Solana Calabro, CHt., a graduate of Syracuse University and Long Island University with degrees in Education and Educational Technology. She has had over 34 years of teaching experience at the middle and high school levels, in addition to 20 years as a staff development trainer. She is life long learner, educator, mentor and Mom.

She resides in Northern California. When she is not tapping or practicing Hypnosis, you will find her writing, knitting or just enjoying the beauty around her.

www.hypnosislifelearning.com
www.tapforteachers.com
www.taptoachieve.com

www.ingramcontent.com/pod-product-compliance
Lightning Source LLC
Chambersburg PA
CBHW061346040426
42444CB00011B/3114